AMPHIBIANS

BookLife

GRACE JONES

Words that appear like **this** can be found in the glossary on page 24.

©2016
Book Life
King's Lynn
Norfolk PE30 4LS

ISBN: 978-1-78637-028-0

All rights reserved
Printed in Spain

Written by:
Grace Jones

Designed by:
Ian McMullen

contents

What are Living Things?

All living things move and grow. Living things need air, food, water and sunlight to stay alive.

These are all living things.

Frog

Tiger

Human

Knife, fork & plate.

Books

These are all non-living things.

Non-living things do not move or grow. Non-living things do not need air, food, water or sunlight because they are not alive.

Teddy Bear

What is an Amphibian?

Amphibians are living things that can live in the water and on land. They need air, food, water and sunlight to live. Frogs, salamanders and toads are all types of amphibians.

Frog

Toad

Salamander

Amphibians usually have four legs and webbed feet. They are cold-blooded animals. This means that their body temperature changes when the temperature outside is hotter or colder.

Legs

Webbed Feet

Fact: There are over 7,000 known species of amphibian.

Where do they Live?

All living things live in a **habitat** or home. Amphibians live near to water or in damp places, including streams, forests, meadows, bogs, swamps, ponds, rainforests and lakes.

Forest

Most amphibians live in the water when they are very young. This is because they do not yet have lungs to be able to breathe air on land or legs to walk with.

Young frogs, called tadpoles.

Amphibian Homes

Amphibians live in many different habitats around the world. A common habitat for frogs and toads are freshwater ponds. The reeds provide them with shelter from **predators** and the insects in the pond provide them with food to eat.

Some amphibians live in hotter **climates**, such as rainforests. Rainforests get a lot of rain every year, providing a wet climate for amphibians to live in.

What do they Eat?

Nearly all adult amphibians are **carnivores**. They mostly eat insects, worms, slugs and even small animals, like mice. They use their super sense of smell to hunt out prey at night-time.

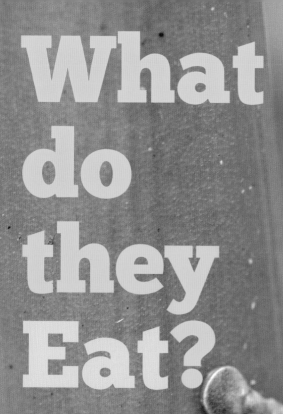

The Brazilian Tree frog is the only known frog to eat fruits and berries.

Amphibians have long, sticky tongues which they use to catch their food. They also have strong back legs so they can jump quickly and take their **prey** by surprise.

Strong Back Legs

Sticky Tongue

Fact:
Amphibians don't need to drink any water because they take it in through their skin.

A Red-Eyed Tree frog sticks out his tongue to catch a butterfly.

How do they Breathe?

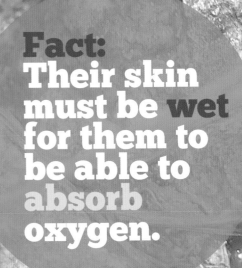

Most amphibians breathe through their lungs and their skin. Oxygen is absorbed through the skin and then moves around the rest of the body.

Fact:
Their skin must be wet for them to be able to absorb oxygen.

Tadpoles

Gills

Some amphibians, like tadpoles, have gills on either side of their bodies which they use to breathe with under the water. When they are older, they grow lungs which lets them breathe on land too.

How do they Move?

Long Body

Fire Salamander

Tail

Short Legs

Amphibians with tails, like salamanders, usually have long bodies and short, weak legs. This means that they can't run very quickly and move in a similar way to a snake.

16

Tailless amphibians, like frogs and toads, have short, wider bodies and strong back legs. Their back legs are usually three times larger than their front legs, which means they can jump very high.

No Tail

Short Body

Strong
Back Legs

Jumping
Pacman
Frog

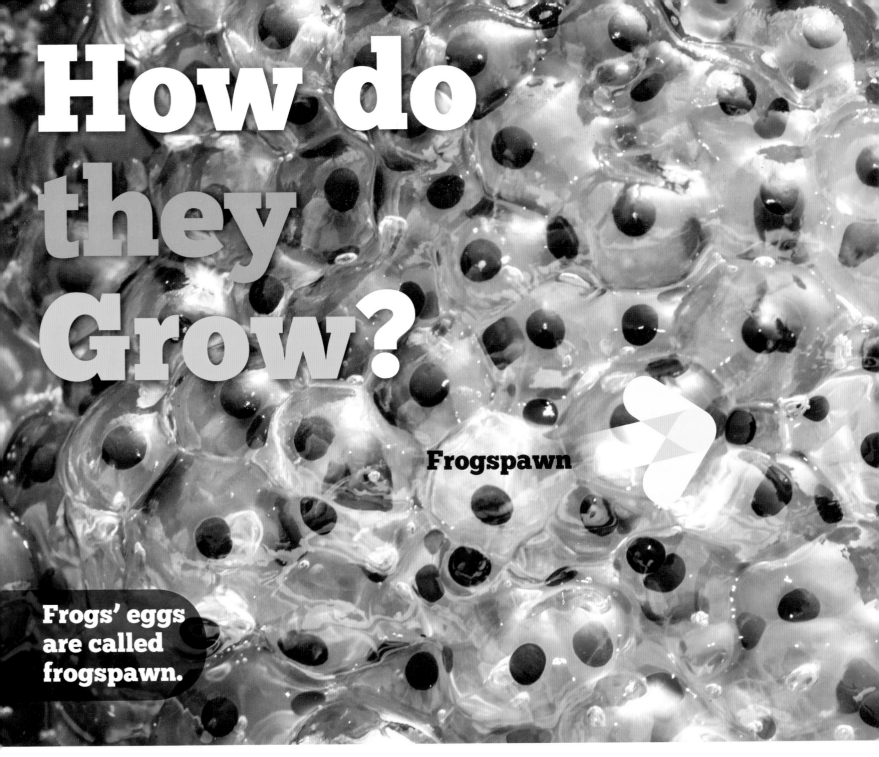

How do they Grow?

Frogspawn

Frogs' eggs are called frogspawn.

Most amphibians start life as eggs that **hatch** into tadpoles or **larvae** that live in water. At this stage, they eat lots of plant food so they can grow big and strong.

The young amphibians begin to grow lungs so they can breathe on land and eat animals or insects instead of plants. They continue to grow and change until they are fully-grown adults. This can take anywhere from a few weeks to more than a year.

A newly hatched salamander.

An adult Blue-Spotted Salamander.

Amazing
Amphibians

Amphibians can be very colourful. The Red-Eyed Tree frog lives in the rainforests of South America and has red eyes, orange toes and a green and blue body.

Fact:
A group of frogs is called an 'army'.

The frogs' brightly coloured skin warns other animals that it is poisonous or dangerous if eaten. This stops them being eaten by predators.

Some female salamanders lay their eggs on land and protect
them until they hatch. Whilst they are looking after their eggs,
the mothers do not eat or sleep.

World Record Breakers

CHINESE GIANT SALAMANDER

Record:
The World's Biggest Amphibian

Fact:
Chinese Giant salamanders live in lakes in China and are bigger than most sharks!

Size:
Up to 180cm long

GLASS **FROG**

Record:
The World's Weirdest Amphibian

Fact:
The Glass Frog is completely see through. What can you see inside the frog?

Size:
2cm long

2cm
Actual size!

Glossary

Carnivores: animals that eat other animals rather than plants.

Climates: types of weather in particular places.

Habitat: a home where animals and plants live.

Hatch: when a baby animal or insect comes out of its egg.

Larvae: an insect or animal's young.

Predators: any animal that eats other animals and insects.

Prey: any animal or insect that is eaten by another.

Index

Photo Credits